Anxiety Disorders Interview Schedule for DSM-IV

Adult and Lifetime Version

Clinician Manual

Timothy A. Brown
Peter A. DiNardo
David H. Barlow

OXFORD
UNIVERSITY PRESS

OXFORD
UNIVERSITY PRESS

Oxford University Press, Inc., publishes works that further
Oxford University's objective of excellence
in research, scholarship, and education.

Oxford New York
Auckland Cape Town Dar es Salaam Hong Kong Karachi
Kuala Lumpur Madrid Melbourne Mexico City Nairobi
New Delhi Shanghai Taipei Toronto

With offices in
Argentina Austria Brazil Chile Czech Republic France Greece
Guatemala Hungary Italy Japan Poland Portugal Singapore
South Korea Switzerland Thailand Turkey Ukraine Vietnam

Published by Oxford University Press, Inc.
198 Madison Avenue, New York, New York 10016

www.oup.com

Oxford is a registered trademark of Oxford University Press

ISBN 978-0-19-518388-7

9 8 7

Printed in the United States of America
on acid-free paper

ABOUT THE AUTHORS

Timothy A. Brown received his PsyD from the Virginia Consortium for Professional Psychology in 1988. He has published numerous scientific articles and chapters in the area of anxiety disorders. Presently, he is associate director of the Center for Anxiety and Related Disorders at Boston University and research associate/professor in the psychology department at Boston University. He has been a consultant to the National Institute of Mental Health on the evaluation of psychosocial and pharmacological treatments for anxiety disorders, and he has served as a consultant for large-scale projects focusing on the assessment and diagnosis of anxiety disorders using DSM–IV criteria. In addition, he was a member of the DSM–IV Anxiety Disorders Sub-Workgroup for generalized anxiety disorders and mixed anxiety depression. Recently, his research has focused on the classification of anxiety disorders, the development and evaluation of short- and long-term outcome of psychosocial treatments for anxiety disorders, and the nature and assessment of panic and generalized anxiety disorder.

Peter A. DiNardo received his PhD in Clinical Psychology from Washington University in 1974. He is presently professor of psychology at the State University of New York, College at Oneonta, and he has been a consultant to the Phobia and Anxiety Disorders Clinic at the Center for Stress and Anxiety Disorders since 1982. His current research interests include diagnostic reliability of DSM–IV anxiety disorders and etiological factors in specific phobias.

David H. Barlow received his PhD from the University of Vermont in 1969, and he has published 15 books and more than 200 articles and chapters, mostly in the areas of anxiety disorders, sexual problems, and clinical research methodology. His recent books include *Clinical Handbook of Psychological Disorders: A Step-by-Step Treatment Manual—Second Edition* (1993), *Anxiety and Its Disorders: The Nature and Treatment of Anxiety and Panic* (1988), and *Mastery of Your Anxiety and Panic—Second Edition and Agoraphobia Supplement Therapist Guide,* coauthored by Michelle Craske (1994). Dr. Barlow was formerly professor of psychiatry and psychology at Brown University and Distinguished Professor in the Department of Psychology at the University at Albany–State University of New York. Currently, he is professor of psychology, director of the Clinical Training Program, and director of the Center for Anxiety and Related Disorders at Boston University. Dr. Barlow is also past president of the Division of Clinical Psychology of the American Psychological Association. He has been a consultant to the National Institute of Mental Health (NIMH) and the National Institutes of Health since 1973 and was recently awarded a merit award from the NIMH for "research competence and productivity that are distinctly superior." He was a member of the DSM–IV Task Force. The major objective of his work for the last 15 years has been the development of new treatments for anxiety disorders.

Introduction

The Anxiety Disorders Interview Schedule for DSM-IV (ADIS-IV; Brown, Di Nardo, & Barlow, 1994) is a structured interview designed to assess for current episodes of anxiety disorders, and to permit differential diagnosis among the anxiety disorders according to DSM-IV criteria (American Psychiatric Association, 1994). The ADIS-IV also provides sufficient information to permit functional analysis of the anxiety disorders. In addition, sections to assess current mood, somatoform, and substance use disorders are included because of their high comorbidity rate with anxiety disorders and because the presenting symptomatology of these disorders is often quite similar to that of the anxiety disorders. The ADIS-IV also contains screening questions for psychotic and conversion symptoms and familial psychiatric history. A more detailed section is included to ascertain the patient's medical and psychiatric treatment history. Finally, with the exception of Axis II disorders, the ADIS-IV permits the use of the DSM-IV multiaxial system.

The Anxiety Disorders Interview Schedule for DSM-IV: Lifetime Version (ADIS-IV-L; Di Nardo, Brown, & Barlow, 1994) contains all of the sections included in the ADIS-IV. However, unlike the ADIS-IV, the ADIS-IV-L has been designed to establish past (lifetime) diagnoses as well. The ADIS-IV-L also contains a Diagnostic Timeline to assist in the determination of the onset, remission, and temporal sequence of disorders. This manual has been developed to accompany both the ADIS-IV and ADIS-IV-L. Because the ADIS-IV and the ADIS-IV-L differ only in that the latter contains sections to assess for past diagnoses, the abbreviation "ADIS-IV" will be used throughout the manual in discussing information germane to both schedules. When discussing issues specific to the ADIS-IV-L, the abbreviation "ADIS-IV-L" will be used.

Because the ADIS-IV is designed for the detailed examination of the anxiety disorders and related problems, it will be of most value for research and clinical applications directly related to these problem areas. More comprehensive structured interviews may be better suited for general outpatient clinics or more broad-based research efforts that aim to evaluate all of the DSM-IV disorders. For these purposes, we recommend the updated version of the Structured Clinical Interview for DSM-III-R (SCID-R; Spitzer, Williams, Gibbon, & First, 1992). However, such interviews provide a considerably less detailed evaluation of the anxiety disorders than does the ADIS-IV.

The ADIS-IV and its predecessors, the ADIS and the ADIS-R, have been developed over a period of years in a clinical research center for the anxiety disorders that is supported in part by funds from the National Institute for Mental Health. The content and wording of questions, as well as the general organization of the interview, are based on several years of experience in interviewing and diagnosing patients with anxiety disorders. Previous editions of the ADIS have demonstrated good reliability for the majority of disorders covered (Di Nardo, O'Brien, Barlow, Waddell, & Blanchard, 1983). In a recent article (Di Nardo, Moras, Barlow, Rapee, & Brown, 1993), test-retest reliability for the DSM-III-R anxiety disorders ranged from .57 to .82 when the ADIS-R was used as the diagnostic instrument.

Uses of the ADIS-IV

Clinical applications. Over the past several years, psychosocial and pharmacological treatments for the anxiety disorders have become increasingly specific. Thus, before treatment planning can be initiated, it is important to obtain a comprehensive evaluation of the presenting complaint and any co-occurring disorders, both psychological and medical. The ADIS-IV has been developed to facilitate differential diagnosis among the anxiety disorders and commonly co-occurring disorders. This inquiry also enables the clinician to understand the functional relationships among these disorders and their associated symptomatology. Particularly in the area of the anxiety disorders, many of the questions go beyond establishing the basic diagnostic criteria and focus on the functional relationships among specific symptoms. For instance, there are many symptoms that cut across all of the anxiety disorders: e.g., panic attacks, social anxiety, worry (anxious apprehension), and situational avoidance. Moreover, many patients with anxiety disorders present with more than one disorder, referred to as comorbidity (cf. Brown & Barlow, 1992; Di Nardo & Barlow, 1990). DSM-IV allows for multiple diagnoses, following certain exclusionary rules. For example, generalized anxiety disorder (GAD) can be assigned in the presence of other Axis I disorders, provided that the focus of anxiety and worry is not confined to features of another Axis I disorder and the disturbance does not occur exclusively during a mood disorder, psychotic disorder, or a pervasive developmental disorder. Thus, a potential issue for differential diagnosis involving GAD is to determine if all of the symptoms reported by the patient can be subsumed under a co-occurring disorder or whether the symptoms form another, independent disorder.

Even for purely clinical applications, we favor a structured interview format such as the ADIS-IV for differential diagnosis because it ensures the systematic inquiry necessary to determine the relationships among anxiety symptoms. In each diagnostic section of the ADIS-IV, there are questions designed to determine if the patient meets the diagnostic criteria for that disorder, the exact focus of concern associated with each symptom, and the relationship of the symptom to symptoms reported by the patient in other diagnostic sections. Systematic and detailed questioning of this nature is necessary for reliable differential diagnosis.

Research applications. In clinical research, it is essential that the methods used to diagnose patients for inclusion in the study have demonstrated reliability and validity. Therefore, a structured interview is needed to reduce information variance and interviewer variance, and to ensure replicability of diagnostic procedures. In addition to items assessing the basic diagnostic criteria, the ADIS-IV includes a number of questions designed to provide a systematic and quantifiable assessment of the various dimensional aspects of the disorder. In most diagnostic sections, the initial screening questions are linked to the key feature of the disorder, and have been designed to be rated on a dichotomous basis (i.e., yes/no). After the initial screening items, the inquiry proceeds to symptom ratings that are also linked to the key feature(s) of the disorder, but these ratings are made on a dimensional basis (i.e., 0-8 scales) rather than on a dichotomous basis. This method of inquiry is based, in part, on findings that certain symptoms are found in all of the anxiety disorders and other Axis I disorders, as well as in normal subjects. Thus, these dimensional ratings may be more conducive to certain research applications such as comparisons among diagnostic groups on selected clinical features or for use as indices of treatment outcome.

In addition, some diagnostic sections are followed by research sections that are intended to gather information that may be useful for a variety of research applications (e.g., nocturnal panic, vulnerability factors, discriminant validity). The research sections are not necessary for diagnosis and thus are optional.

Coverage of the ADIS-IV

As noted earlier, the ADIS-IV is designed primarily for detailed assessment and diagnosis of the anxiety disorders. Thus, diagnostic sections for the anxiety disorders are presented first. These sections contain the most detailed inquiry including items necessary to evaluate each DSM-IV diagnostic criterion for the disorder and questions that facilitate differential diagnosis. In addition, diagnostic sections for the mood, somatoform, and substance use disorders are included. These sections also permit full diagnosis (and differential diagnosis) on the basis of DSM-IV criteria. The brief screening items for psychotic and conversion symptoms are included for clinical purposes and because these symptoms are often part of exclusion criteria in research protocols (i.e., psychoses, conversion reactions, and somatoform pain reaction). Relative to its predecessors, the ADIS-IV contains fairly detailed sections on the patient's medical and treatment history as this information is often very important for diagnosis and treatment planning.

The 24-item Hamilton Rating Scale for Depression (HRSD; Hamilton, 1960) and the 14-item Hamilton Anxiety Rating Scale (HARS; Hamilton, 1959) are included at the end of the ADIS-IV and instructions for the administration of these scales are provided in Appendix A of this manual. These rating scales provide a detailed evaluation the current level of depressive and anxious symptomatology, and can be used for a variety of purposes (e.g., treatment outcome measures, between-groups comparisons among clinical samples). The Hamilton scales are not necessary to establish DSM-IV diagnoses and may be omitted.

The ADIS-IV begins by gathering typical demographic data (e.g., education, marital status, occupation history, religious affiliation, information on the spouse/significant other). Next, a brief description of the presenting problem is obtained, which provides the interviewer with a general sense of the problem areas to be pursued in more detail and establishes a common reference point for interviewer and patient. Next, the interviewer should record a verbatim response to the question, "What would you say is the main reason that brought you here today?" The patient's response to this question may be helpful later in establishing a principal diagnosis and may be useful for certain research applications. This inquiry is followed by a brief evaluation of changes in or difficulties with several areas of life circumstances within the past year (e.g., work/school, family/relationships, finances). This provides an opportunity to obtain a broad overview of the patient's life circumstances. This information is important for establishing a context for the current symptomatology and may be helpful for diagnostic purposes (e.g., consideration of the adjustment disorders). Moreover, these data may provide information regarding the reason for the current presentation, and provide a basis for assessment of current life stressors (Axis IV) and overall level of functioning (Axis V).

Assessment of specific Axis I disorders follows these introductory sections and begins with the anxiety disorders. The order in which the diagnostic sections for the anxiety disorders are presented was guided in part to facilitate continuity (e.g., presentation of the Agoraphobia section after the Panic Disorder section) and to facilitate differential diagnosis (e.g., juxtaposition of the Generalized Anxiety Disorder and Obsessive-Compulsive Disorder sections). The diagnostic section for Panic Disorder appears first due to the fact that this disorder is the most frequently encountered anxiety disorder in many settings and because panic attacks can appear in the context of any anxiety disorder. Agoraphobia follows this section. Social Phobia follows these sections because social anxiety and avoidance is often part of the associated symptomatology of Agoraphobia. Generalized Anxiety Disorder (GAD) follows, helping the interviewer to separate GAD-related worry from worry related to panic or social phobia concerns. Obsessive-Compulsive Disorder follows the GAD section, which may assist in differentiating GAD excessive worry from obsessional thoughts. The diagnostic section for Specific Phobia is next. A commonly encountered issue in the differential diagnosis of specific phobia is determining whether the anxiety or avoidance of specific objects or situations could be subsumed under the symptomatology of other disorders such as panic disorder with agoraphobia (e.g., fear of air travel is due to apprehension of having unexpected panic attacks that occur in a variety of situational contexts). The diagnostic section for Posttraumatic Stress Disorder and Acute Stress Disorder is the last anxiety disorder to be covered, reflecting in part the desirability of reserving potentially sensitive questions concerning traumatic events for a point in the interview when it is more likely that good rapport has been established.

The next diagnostic sections are devoted to the mood disorders, with detailed sections for Major Depression, Dysthymia, and Mania/Cyclothymia. As noted earlier, these sections are somewhat less detailed than the sections on the anxiety disorders but nonetheless provide sufficient detail to establish current and past DSM-IV diagnoses. Following the mood disorders, there are diagnostic sections for two somatoform disorders (Hypochondriasis and Somatization Disorder). The Hypochondriasis section offers a comprehensive assessment of current and past episodes of this disorder; the Somatization Disorder section provides an assessment for current episodes only.

The diagnostic section for Mixed Anxiety Depression (MAD) follows. This diagnosis is not an official Axis I disorder, but appears in Appendix B of DSM-IV (Criteria Sets and Axes Provided for Further Study). Under DSM-IV guidelines, patients meeting the diagnostic criteria for MAD would be formally assigned the diagnosis, Anxiety Disorder NOS. Thus, although this section is not necessary for assigning official DSM-IV diagnoses, it may be of use in primary care settings where patients may present with atypical anxiety or mood symptoms. In addition, the MAD section may be useful for research purposes. MAD cannot be assigned if the patient currently meets diagnostic criteria for any current anxiety or mood disorder and certain adjustment disorders, or if the patient has a past diagnosis of GAD, major depression, dysthymia, or panic disorder. Therefore, it is a diagnosis of exclusion and is assessed only after all of the anxiety and mood disorder diagnostic sections have been administered.

Following the MAD section are diagnostic sections that allow for the evaluation of current and past substance use disorders (alcohol and other substances are presented in two separate sections). These sections are followed by items for psychotic and conversion symptoms and family history of psychological disorders. These items are intended for screening purposes only and are not sufficient for establishing DSM-IV diagnoses. Next is the section to ascertain the patient's psychological/psychiatric treatment history and medical history.

The Hamilton Scales have been placed at the end of the ADIS-IV; thus, these scales are administered after all of the major diagnostic sections have been completed. Accordingly, the interviewer has already obtained a comprehensive evaluation of the patient's presenting symptomatology. Administration of the Hamilton Scales entails the assessment of the frequency and severity of symptoms using the past month as the time frame (although the inquiry can be readily adapted for different time frames). By administering these scales, the interviewer can make an assessment of current levels of general anxious and depressive symptomatology that cut across the specific diagnoses. Ideally, the Hamilton ratings are established by making a specific inquiry for each item; however, they can be made on the basis of the patient's responses to previous diagnostic sections.

Organization of Diagnostic Sections

The ADIS-IV provides for detailed inquiry for all aspects of the DSM-IV criteria for the disorders mentioned above, and suggested phrasing of questions appears in **bold print** throughout the protocol. The diagnostic sections of the ADIS-IV have been structured to be as consistent as possible. Each section begins with INITIAL INQUIRY, which typically contains dichotomous items (yes/no) that have been designed to assess the key feature(s) of the disorder. The screening items assess for current and then past occurrences of these key diagnostic features. Depending on the patient's response to these items, the interviewer may then make several inquiries designed to ascertain whether separate instances of this symptomatology may have occurred previously. These items alone are not intended to establish the presence of current and past episodes of the disorder, but are intended to provide the interviewer with a sense of how the diagnostic section might proceed. In many of the anxiety disorder sections, these dichotomous items are followed by dimensional ratings of current and past occurrences of the key feature(s) of the disorder. Information obtained from these dimensional ratings will more clearly establish the presence or absence of the key feature(s) of the disorder. The first formal skip-out instructions for the diagnostic section are often located immediately following these dimensional ratings.

Unlike the ADIS-IV-L, the ADIS-IV does not contain separate sections for inquiry of past disorders. Nevertheless, the ADIS-IV contains a screening item for past episodes in INITIAL INQUIRY (as well as another item at the end of the CURRENT EPISODE section), so that the clinician may inquire about the possible presence of past disorders. Depending on the patient's response to these items, the clinician may wish to adapt the CURRENT EPISODE section to inquire about previous disorders. This may be particularly useful if the existence of past disorders has a potential impact on current presentation or differential diagnosis (e.g., mixed anxiety depression should not be diagnosed if a past diagnosis of major depression exists).

The second section is CURRENT EPISODE, which contains all of the items necessary for establishing a current DSM-IV diagnosis as well as many items to assist in differential diagnosis (e.g., whether the symptoms might be due to a medical condition or the effects of a substance). Often, the items in this section that are linked to a diagnostic criterion begin in an open-ended manner and then "funnel" down to the specific content of the criterion. For example, questions relating to the duration of symptomatology often begin as "How often has _____ been present?" The patient's initial response to this question may be clear enough to determine whether the temporal criterion has been met. If not, the follow-up questions include specific reference to the exact timeframe specified in DSM-IV. For instance, DSM-IV criteria for panic disorder require one month of persistent worry about the attacks or their consequences, or a change in behavior related to the panics. The initial inquiry for the persistent worry aspect of this criterion is open-ended. If the patient's response does not clearly establish that there has been at least a month of worry, a follow-up question asks, "Since your first attack, has there been a period of a month or more when you were worried that you might have more attacks?"

Towards the end of the CURRENT EPISODE section, there are several questions that are intended to ascertain the date of onset of the disorder as well as factors that may have had etiological significance in the emergence of the disorder (e.g., stressful life events). In establishing the onset of a disorder (and remission of a disorder in the PAST EPISODE section of the ADIS-IV-L), the items in this section are intended to distinguish between the emergence of the "features" of the disorder and the onset of the disorder itself (i.e., the date in which the symptoms constituted a diagnosable condition which, by DSM-IV definition, may entail when the symptoms were persistent, recurrent, and/or associated with clinically significant distress or impairment). Many patients, when questioned about the onset of a problem, will relate this question to the beginning of the symptoms rather than to when the symptoms met diagnostic threshold for a DSM-IV disorder. For example, patients with panic disorder may relate the onset of their problem to their initial panic attack which may or may not have constituted the beginning of their panic disorder. Additionally, patients with generalized anxiety disorder often report that they have been worriers all of their lives. However, closer questioning reveals that the worry did not create significant distress or impairment until a more recent time, perhaps in response to a specific change in life circumstances. Accordingly, the ADIS-IV question regarding onset is phrased to highlight the aspects of the symptomatology that constitute the diagnostic threshold for the DSM-IV disorder. Phrased in this way, the question more firmly establishes the onset of the disorder. In each diagnostic section, it is suggested that when the patient is vague in relating the date of onset, that a more specific date of onset might be obtained by having the patient associate the time of onset to objective life events in which the date is known (e.g., marriage, graduation, start of job, etc.). For clinical and research purposes where the temporal sequence of disorders or dates of onset and remission of disorders needs to be established even more precisely, the ADIS-IV-L contains a Diagnostic Timeline (DTL) that should be administered at the end of the interview. The specific instructions for the administration of the DTL may be found in Appendix B of this manual.

In both the ADIS-IV and ADIS-IV-L, the CURRENT EPISODE section is usually concluded by an item ascertaining whether past episodes of the same disorder may have existed. Although a similar item has been previously administered in the INITIAL INQUIRY section, it appears again here because the interviewer now has a firm sense of whether the patient currently meets diagnostic criteria for the disorder in question. With this knowledge, the interviewer can establish whether a separate, prior episode has occurred with greater certainty.

In the ADIS-IV-L, the section for PAST EPISODE is located after the CURRENT EPISODE section. (Of course, if the patient's responses to the items in INITIAL INQUIRY indicate the presence of a past disorder only, the interviewer would skip over the CURRENT EPISODE section). In most cases, this section is identical to the CURRENT EPISODE section with the exception that the items have been altered to the past tense. The only additional items that occur in all diagnostic sections concern the assessment of the date of remission of the disorder and factors that may have been related to the remission.

Administering the ADIS-IV

General considerations. Although all attempts have been made to make the ADIS-IV as detailed and explicit as possible, any clinical interview will require further elaboration by the patient on some items. Often, the interviewer will need to exercise clinical judgment to determine if further inquiry is necessary, and to ascertain whether the patient's response satisfies the diagnostic criterion. Thus, it is critical that the interviewer be familiar not only with the ADIS-IV protocol and this manual, but with DSM-IV. This also implies that, although items presented in bold-face type represent the suggested phrasing of the inquiry, clinical judgment may be necessary to determine if the item can be administered as worded or whether the item should be re-phrased to meet the demands of the patient or to maintain continuity of the interview session. For example, depending on the intellectual or educational characteristics of the patient, some items in the ADIS-IV may need to be reworded due to the reading level or length of the item. Similarly, as the interview progresses, symptoms that the patient may have endorsed in prior sections of the ADIS-IV may overlap with symptom inquiry in subsequent sections (e.g., administration of screening items for Dysthymia following the Major Depression diagnostic section). In many instances, there are specific questions in the diagnostic sections that address these relationships, and the interviewer can alter the wording of some questions to reflect the fact that prior inquiry has been made for these symptoms. For example, if it has been previously established that the patient meets diagnostic criteria for panic disorder, the initial screening item in the generalized anxiety disorder section might be re-phrased by asking: "Other than the worry that you have about having panic attacks, over the last several months, have you been continually worried or anxious about a number of events or activities in your daily life?"

In some sections (e.g., Panic Disorder), it is possible to reach an ADIS-IV skip-out after only a few dichotomous items have been administered. In these instances, some elaboration or clarification of the patient's initial response may be necessary to determine whether a positive or negative rating is warranted. When establishing dimensional ratings within the INITIAL INQUIRY section or when administering the items contained in CURRENT and PAST EPISODES, clinical judgment is often necessary to determine the extent to which additional inquiry beyond the items presented in the ADIS-IV is needed to record the most accurate response (e.g., ascertaining whether the patient's symptom endorsement relates to the disorder in question or whether these symptoms relate to a co-occurring disorder; determining if the patient is differentiating past and current episodes adequately; determining if the patient comprehends the question sufficiently).

During the CURRENT EPISODE section (as well as the section for PAST EPISODE), clinical judgment is necessary to determine whether the remainder of the section can be skipped if the patient's responses indicate that the diagnostic criteria are not met. For example, in a patient who has responded affirmatively to the initial questions for social phobia, and who shows some current anxiety and avoidance of social situations from responses to the dimensional items contained in INITIAL INQUIRY, inquiry should proceed to the CURRENT EPISODE section.

If questioning in this section reveals a negligible degree of distress or interference associated with the social concerns, the interviewer may decide to omit the remaining questions.

Establishing current and past diagnoses. The ADIS-IV-L differs from its predecessors in that it provides for detailed inquiry for past episodes of most disorders covered in the protocol. In cases in which there has been only a past episode of the disorder, the CURRENT EPISODE section and corresponding dimensional ratings in INITIAL INQUIRY may be used to assist in establishing criteria for full or partial remission after the PAST EPISODE section has been administered.

As noted earlier, in most diagnostic sections the last dichotomous items in INITIAL INQUIRY are intended to permit the interviewer to make an initial determination of whether the key features of the disorder have been present continuously, or if there have been discrete episodes, separated by periods of remission. Anxiety and mood disorders often have a fluctuating course and the interviewer must attempt to determine if there have been discrete episodes of a disturbance, as opposed to the continuation of a longstanding episode with fluctuations in the severity and/or persistency of symptoms. Such fluctuations should not be considered as separate episodes unless the inquiry establishes a significant period of time during which the patient was symptom free, or there was a very clear remission. In addition to the initial screening questions concerning the presence of separate, past episodes, the additional questions residing in the CURRENT and PAST EPISODE sections are provided to assist the interviewer in making this determination.

During the initial inquiry, the interviewer should establish a rough timeframe for the onset and remission of the symptoms, and refer to this timeframe during the CURRENT and PAST EPISODE sections that follow. If there is evidence of multiple episodes initially, the interviewer should take care to indicate to the patient the particular episode to which the questions refer. The questions in the diagnostic sections have suggested phrasing to assist the interviewer in this inquiry.

In two diagnostic sections, Panic Disorder and Major Depression, the ADIS-IV-L provides space to record two past episodes of the disorder. Although it would have made the ADIS-IV-L overly lengthy to do this for each disorder, panic disorder and major depression are afforded space to record two past episodes because these disorders were considered the most likely to be characterized by multiple remissions and recurrences. In the Major Depression section, when the patient indicates the presence of more than one past episode, it is suggested that the interviewer first inquire about the episode that the patient deems to be the worst. Potentially, this strategy will allow the interviewer to first determine whether the patient has ever met diagnostic criteria for DSM-IV major depressive disorder; the subsequent inquiry about other episodes may then be performed more efficiently (e.g., consideration of recurrent vs. single episode).

Although it may be occur less frequently than for panic disorder and major depression, the interviewer will encounter cases of multiple past episodes of disorders where the ADIS-IV-L provides space to record a single past episode. In these instances, the interview should be adapted to meet the diagnostician's requirements, whether they be clinical or empirical. For example, the diagnostician may opt to inquire about the worst, first, or most recent episode, or for research purposes, may decide to inquire about all prior episodes by adapting the protocol or by using copies of PAST EPISODE sections from other protocols. For clinical purposes, it may be important to inquire about the episode that the patient regards as the worst episode in instances where it is not clear that the diagnostic threshold has ever been met. In other cases, it may be important to inquire about a past episode whose onset appears to be contiguous with the emergence of another disorder, for the purposes of differential diagnosis and to ascertain if diagnostic hierarchy rules apply.

Assigning diagnoses. Immediately following the Hamilton scales, the two final questions appear: the first asks the patient what is the primary problem that they want help with; the second asks whether the patient feels that there is any other material that should be discussed that has yet to be covered. The first item is very similar to the question asked near the beginning of the interview. However, it is not uncommon to observe variability in the patient's response to this item once all of the diagnostic sections have been completed. These responses may be helpful to the interviewer in the determination of the patient's principal diagnosis (see below). Following these items, the ADIS-IV provides space for information on mental status, behavior during the interview, and a diagnostic narrative, to be recorded by the interviewer after the patient has departed.

On the following page, CLINICIAN'S RATINGS AND DIAGNOSES, the diagnostician is to record the DSM-IV five-axis diagnosis. In addition, space is provided to record past diagnoses and their respective dates of onset and remission, scores on the Hamilton Anxiety and Depression scales, and the duration of the interview. Finally, the interviewer provides a diagnostic confidence rating (0-100 scale, where 100 reflects complete certainty), which is a global rating to reflect the interviewer's overall confidence in the accuracy of the five-axis diagnosis. When the interviewer assigns a rating of 70 or less, space is provided to comment on the factors associated with the uncertainty (e.g., "patient's report was quite inconsistent," "difficulty in establishing the diagnostic boundary between social avoidance and agoraphobic avoidance").

Each current and past diagnosis that is listed should be assigned a separate ADIS-IV clinical severity rating using the 0-8 scale that appears at the top of the page. This rating should reflect the degree of distress/interference associated with the diagnosis. Thus, this rating differs from the Axis V GAF rating which is intended to be an index of the patient's overall level of functioning. Accordingly, the diagnostician would assign a separate ADIS-IV clinical severity rating for each diagnosis. In instances where more than one diagnosis is assigned, the disorder recorded as the "principal diagnosis" is the disorder responsible for the greatest level of distress or interference in functioning (i.e., the disorder with the highest ADIS-IV clinical severity rating). If other disorders are present but are not as problematic (i.e., have lower clinical severity ratings), they are listed as "additional diagnoses." It is important to note that a longer-standing disorder is not necessarily the disorder that is assigned as the "principal diagnosis." However, the interviewer may occasionally determine that two or more diagnoses exist that are equally problematic; in such cases, the diagnoses would be assigned the same clinical severity rating and would be recorded as "co-principal diagnoses."

Based on conventions developed at the Phobia and Anxiety Disorders Clinic, the ADIS-IV clinical severity ratings are used to distinguish clinical and subclinical diagnoses. Accordingly, severity ratings of 4 or above signify that the patient's symptomatology meets or surpasses the diagnostic threshold to qualify as a DSM-IV disorder (i.e., all the diagnostic criteria for the disorder have been met). Subclinical diagnoses are assigned severity ratings of 3 or less. For example, symptomatology that has always been just under the DSM-IV diagnostic threshold might be given a severity rating of 3. A clinical example of this would be a person who has a prominent fear of spiders but has never met the DSM-IV interference/distress criterion for specific phobia (e.g., because the person lives in the city and never encounters spiders). Ratings of 3 or less would also be used in association with diagnoses that are in full or partial remission. In treatment outcome studies where the ADIS-IV is used, the clinical severity rating is often used as an index of improvement at post-treatment and follow-up assessment.

Diagnostic Timeline. The final page of the ADIS-IV-L contains the Diagnostic Timeline (DTL). The purpose of the DTL is to refine, review, and otherwise obtain more specific information regarding the age of onset/remission and relative sequence of past and current disorders and corresponding life events. The DTL is administered after the interviewer has covered all diagnostic sections of the ADIS-IV-L. Thus, at the point that the DTL is conducted, the interviewer has determined which current and past disorders to inquire about and has a sense of their approximate dates of onset/remission. The DTL has been developed primarily for research purposes where it is important to collect specific data on such issues as the temporal sequence of disorders or factors relating to the onset/remission of disorders (e.g., life events). Instructions for the administration of the DTL are found in Appendix B.

Establishing Differential Diagnoses: Some Examples

Throughout the previous sections, it has been noted that considerable clinical knowledge and judgment is necessary to administer structured interviews proficiently and to establish diagnoses accurately. This can be particularly difficult when evaluating patients who present with symptomatology that potentially meets criteria for multiple disorders. In these instances, the interviewer must employ the DSM-IV guidelines to determine which diagnoses are assigned and which are excluded. Often, differential diagnosis is difficult, not only among the anxiety disorders but between the anxiety disorders and "neighboring" disorders (e.g., mood disorders, somatoform disorders). In DSM-IV, the guidelines for such differentiation is explicit, at least more so than in prior versions of the DSM. Within the anxiety disorders, often the basic determination is whether certain symptomatology can be subsumed under the features of another disorder. For example, a diagnosis of specific phobia would be not be warranted in cases where the phobic stimulus is part of the obsessional symptomatology of an obsessive-compulsive disorder. Similarly, avoidance of social situations that has developed as a result of panic disorder would not warrant a social phobia diagnosis. The following examples illustrate the use of some of these guidelines and offer suggestions for the differential diagnosis required by DSM-IV.

Generalized anxiety disorder. In DSM-IV, generalized anxiety disorder (GAD) can be assigned when another Axis I disorder is present if the focus of anxiety or worry is not confined to the features of the co-existing disorder. Thus, differential diagnosis involving GAD may not always be clear particularly in light of findings that patients with GAD usually have at least one additional diagnosis (cf. Brown & Barlow, 1992). For example, patients with GAD frequently have comorbid panic disorder, yet excessive worry about experiencing a panic attack would not constitute a GAD-related worry. Rather, the focus of the anxiety or worry is on a feature of panic disorder (i.e., having additional unexpected panic attacks). Therefore, as specified in DSM-IV, the focus of the patient's anxiety and worry must be unrelated to (and not secondary to) the features of another disorder if a diagnosis of GAD is to be assigned. A second example where this differentiation may be difficult is the area of health concerns. These concerns might be found in GAD, but are often prominent in obsessive-compulsive disorder and particularly in hypochondriasis. However, the health-related worries of patients with GAD patients are often more general and future-oriented in nature, and are less likely to be triggered by a specific class of stimuli or bodily sensations.

Specific phobia. This diagnosis would be contraindicated if the symptomatology is part of another anxiety disorder. For example, an obsessive-compulsive disorder characterized by a fear of contamination might include a phobic avoidance of dirt. If this is the case, a diagnosis of specific phobia of dirt would not be appropriate. Similarly, a fear of heights may be part of a panic disorder with agoraphobia, if being in a tall structure represents a situation in which escape would be difficult in the event of a panic attack.

Differential diagnosis can be difficult in some instances because patients often report several reasons for being fearful of the same situation or object. For example, the patient with panic disorder with agoraphobia might state that he fears and avoids air travel; should this fear be subsumed under the panic disorder or does it constitute a separate diagnosis of specific phobia? Ascertaining the focus(es) of concern should begin to resolve this diagnostic issue. In the aforementioned example, the patient could indicate that he is apprehensive of air travel because: (1) he could have an unexpected panic attack on the plane and be unable to escape; (2) he is extremely concerned that the plane will crash. The presence of the second focus of concern raises the possibility that a separate diagnosis of specific phobia should be assigned. In addition, further inquiry may reveal that the fear of flying had a different point of onset than the panic disorder (e.g., predated the panic disorder by 15 years), thus providing additional support for the independence of the diagnoses under consideration.

DSM-IV has provided a formal typology for three types of panic attacks: unexpected (uncued), situationally bound, and situationally predisposed (cf. Barlow, Brown, & Craske, in press). Under this typology, it is possible that any anxiety disorder (but particularly specific phobia and social phobia) might be appropriately assigned in the presence of panic attacks that the patient experiences as unexpected. In the case of specific phobia or social phobia, these "unexpected" panic attacks would be considered "situationally predisposed" attacks, which are defined in DSM-IV as panic attacks that "are more likely to occur upon exposure to the situational trigger ('cue') but are not invariably associated with the cue." These attacks "may not necessarily occur immediately after the exposure." Thus, the patient who experiences panic attacks when traveling in airplanes, but either does not experience a panic attack each time she flies or cannot predict when the attack will occur during the flight, might be assigned a diagnosis of specific phobia provided that she does not experience unexpected panic attacks in other situational contexts.

Social phobia. As with specific phobia, the diagnosis of social phobia would be contraindicated if the symptomatology is related to the core features of another anxiety disorder.

For example, many patients with panic disorder with agoraphobia avoid social situations because of a fear of panic. In such cases, an additional diagnosis of social phobia is not made. In other cases, the interviewer might judge the social avoidance to be related to an independent social phobia, as in patients who have a history of social avoidance that predates the onset of the panic disorder. An obsessive-compulsive disorder is often associated with avoidance of social situations that might be incorrectly classified as social phobia. An example of this would be the patient who avoids social situations, particularly church, because these situations trigger obsessive urges to shout obscenities. Another example is the patient who evidences extensive avoidance because he is preoccupied with the possibility that he will stare at others' genital areas. This patient may report apprehension of negative social evaluation, but this apprehension is due to his concern that he will get "caught looking." A final example is the patient who avoids crowds due to the fear that she will become contaminated by germs. In all of these examples, a diagnosis of social phobia would not be assigned.

References

American Psychiatric Association (1994). Diagnostic and statistical manual of mental disorders (4th ed.). Washington, DC: Author.

Barlow, D.H., Brown, T.A., & Craske, M.G. (in press). Definitions of panic attacks and panic disorder in DSM-IV: Implications for research. Journal of Abnormal Psychology.

Brown, T.A., & Barlow, D.H. (1992). Comorbidity among anxiety disorders: Implications for treatment and DSM-IV. Journal of Consulting and Clinical Psychology, 60, 835-844.

Brown, T.A., Di Nardo, P.A., & Barlow, D.H. (1994). Anxiety Disorders Interview Schedule for DSM-IV (ADIS-IV). Albany, NY: Graywind Publications Incorporated.

Di Nardo, P.A., & Barlow, D.H. (1990). Syndrome and symptom comorbidity in the anxiety disorders. In J.D. Maser & C.R. Cloninger (Eds.), Comorbidity in anxiety and mood disorders (pp. 205-230). Washington, DC: American Psychiatric Press.

Di Nardo, P.A., Brown, T.A., & Barlow, D.H. (1994). Anxiety Disorders Interview Schedule for DSM-IV: Lifetime Version (ADIS-IV-L). Albany, NY: Graywind Publications Incorporated.

Di Nardo, P.A., Moras, K., Barlow, D.H., Rapee, R.M., & Brown, T.A. (1993). Reliability of DSM-III-R anxiety disorder categories using the Anxiety Disorders Interview Schedule-Revised. Archives of General Psychiatry, 50, 251-256.

Di Nardo, P.A., O'Brien, G.T., Barlow, D.H., Waddell, M.T., & Blanchard, E.B. (1983). Reliability of DSM-III anxiety disorder categories using a new structured interview. Archives of General Psychiatry, 35, 837-844.

Hamilton, M. (1959). The assessment of anxiety states by rating. British Journal of Medical Psychology, 32, 50-55.

Hamilton, M. (1960). A rating scale for depression. Journal of Neurology, Neurosurgery, and Psychiatry, 23, 56-62.

Spitzer, R.L., Williams, J.B.W., Gibbon, M., & First, M.B. (1992). Structured Clinical Interview for DSM-III-R. New York, NY: New York State Psychiatric Institute.

Appendix A

Hamilton Rating Scales

1. All ratings are for the past month.

2. Adjacent Anxiety and Depression items cover similar symptom areas and can be inquired about and rated together. Suggested phrasing for some items appears in **bold type**. Ratings for some items are based on clinical observation rather than on direct inquiry. In all cases, severity rating is based on clinician's judgment.

3. Hamilton Depression items are scored on the basis of the list of descriptors that accompanies each item.

4. Hamilton Anxiety items are rated on a 5-point severity scale:

0	1	2	3	4
None	Mild	Moderate	Severe	Very severe/ Grossly disabling

5. For Hamilton Anxiety items, note that spaces are provided for rating individual symptoms listed under each item. In order to ensure uniformity of information on which Hamilton Anxiety ratings are based, we suggest that the interviewer briefly inquire about and rate the individual symptoms. Each symptom may be rated in the same manner as the items, using the 0-4 severity scale.

Patients who report situational anxiety (e.g., social or specific fears) or panic attacks often experience acute exacerbations of certain anxiety symptoms (palpitations, dyspnea, muscle tension) when exposed to feared situations or during panic. In arriving at ratings for each item, the interviewer should take into account both the patient's general level of symptomatology and the severity of situational/panic symptomatology. For example, if panics or exposures to feared situations are frequent and/or very severe (high intensity or duration of symptoms), the rating should be higher than if the panics or exposures are infrequent or less severe. In this way, the rating of each item will reflect general levels of symptomatology, as well as the frequency and intensity of phobic or panic symptomatology. The severity ratings for individual symptoms are intended to ensure consistency in information gathering, and are to be used for notational purposes only. These ratings should not be added or averaged to derive ratings on the items because the interviewer may give greater weight to symptoms which are a central part of the clinical picture.

For example, on Item 2, a patient may report panic attacks that are characterized by extreme tension and trembling, and that these symptoms are the most intense and disturbing aspects of her panics. When she experiences a panic attack, the tension and trembling often force her to discontinue an ongoing activity. She occasionally feels unable to relax and restless, but these symptoms are not part of the panic attacks. The notations on that item might appear as follows:

Tension:

Feelings of tension	4
Fatigability	0
Inability to relax, keyed up	1
Startle response	0
Moved to tears easily	0
Trembling	4
Feelings of restlessness	1

In this case, the interviewer should assign ratings of 4 to the symptoms of tension and trembling reflecting the central nature of this cluster in her panic attacks. The rating on the entire item might reflect the frequency of panic attacks during the last month: the more frequent the attacks, the higher the severity rating for the item. If the patient reports one or two such panics in the last month, the rating for the item should be 2; if such panics occur on a daily basis, a rating of 4 is made.

Appendix B

Anxiety Disorders Interview Schedule for DSM-IV: Lifetime Version (ADIS-IV-L): Diagnostic Timeline (DTL)

A. Overview

As noted in the text of the manual, the purpose of the DTL is to refine, review, and otherwise obtain more specific information regarding the age of onset/remission and relative sequence of past and current disorders and corresponding life events. The DTL has been developed primarily for research purposes where it is important to collect specific data on such issues as the temporal sequence of disorders or factors relating to the onset/remission of disorders (e.g., life events). However, the DTL may be useful for certain clinical applications (e.g., determination of the temporal sequence of past or current diagnoses for the purposes of differential diagnosis).

B. Procedures

The DTL is administered after the interviewer has covered all diagnostic sections of the ADIS-IV-L. Thus, at the point that the DTL is conducted, the interviewer has determined which current and past disorders to inquire about and has a sense of their approximate dates of onset/remission.

1. As information is subject to revision during the process of completing the DTL, a pencil should be used.

2. Using data obtained from the ADIS-IV-L, record the following on the DTL: (1) in the boxes labeled "DIAG," list all disorders assigned at a clinical severity level of 4 or above in order of their tentative temporal sequence; (2) underneath each diagnosis, list the corresponding date of onset (DOS) and, where appropriate, date of remission (DOR); (3) above each diagnosis, list any precipitating life events (LES-P) noted during the ADIS-IV-L.

3. Plot the patient's date of birth (DOB) and today's date (DATE) on the appropriate ends of the DTL. List the appropriate years over the hash marks on the DTL using whatever interval is appropriate depending on such factors as the patient's age or temporal spacing of the disorders' probable dates of onset and remission.

4. Using data previously obtained during the ADIS-IV-L as well as from the list of examples provided in this Appendix, ascertain and plot several objective life events (LES-O). An LES-O is a life event in which the specific date is known (e.g., marriage, purchase of home, relocation). In particular, try to obtain LES-Os that occurred around the same time as the tentative dates of onset and/or remission of disorders.

5. Usually, it is best to inquire about current disorders prior to trying to refine information concerning past disorders, although exceptions apply often. For example, many times the patient is certain about the onset/remission of their disorders (either current or past) due to their recent onset or remission or due to the fact that the disorder began immediately after an objective life event (e.g., initial panic attack immediately following birth of child, post-traumatic stress reaction precipitated by criminal assault). For disorders in which the patient is definite as to the date of onset and/or remission, obtain the first confidence rating for these dates (CONF #1). Plot dates of all disorders on the DTL for which patient reports a definite date of onset (DOS) and/or date of remission (DOR). If CONF #1 ratings are high (≥ 90%), plot the Preceding Year on DTL. If CONF #1 ratings are low for some dates, use procedures in Step 7. Further refine Precipitating Life Events (LES-P) and record or modify them on the DTL. If necessary, employ shaping questions relating to DOSs and DORs by associating the dates with events (LES-Os and LES-Ps) in which the dates are certain ("So you're sure that your first panic attack occurred after you came back from your trip to Europe but before you started the job at Macy's?").

6. Obtain new confidence ratings for these DOSs and DORs (CONF #2).

7. For disorders in which the DOS or DOR is less certain, begin by asking shaping questions as noted in Step 5 (associating the DOS or DOR both in relation to LES-Os as well as in relation to any disorders in which the DOS, LES-Ps, or perhaps DOR is known). Then, obtain initial confidence ratings for the DOS or DOR (CONF #1). Further refine Precipitating Life Events (LES-P) and record or modify them on the DTL. If necessary, ask further shaping questions relating to the DOSs or DORs provided in relation to life events (LES-Os and LES-Ps) in which the dates are known. Then, obtain new confidence ratings for these DOSs and DORs (CONF #2). If CONF #2 remains low (≤ 70%), decide whether further shaping can be done to assist the patient in recalling the correct dates of onset and/or remission.

8. Repeat the steps above for any past diagnosis that was assigned on the ADIS-IV-L that at one time had a clinical severity of 4 or above.

9. Once all disorders and their corresponding DOSs, DORs, LES-Ps have been plotted, review the entire DTL one more time with the patient to ensure that the information is correct or whether any additional changes are needed (make any revisions necessary).

10. Immediately after the patient has left, the diagnostician should provide their ratings of: (a) confidence in the accuracy of the dates of onset (Rater: OS) and dates of remission (Rater: OR); and (b) Axis IV ratings for each disorder's corresponding LES-Ps (Rater: IV).

A final note on procedures: As in the ADIS-IV-L, the interviewer should be certain to inquire about the DOS of the disorder (i.e., date when the patient's symptomatology met DSM-IV diagnostic criteria) rather then when the features of the disorder first emerged (e.g., the patient's initial panic attack may or may not signify when the onset of panic disorder occurred).

C. A nonexhaustive list of examples of life events (either LES-Ps or LES-Os) that might be included in the DTL procedure

Annual events: holidays (e.g., Christmas, Thanksgiving, New Year's); vacations, end of school year, season of the year, family reunions or get-togethers; non-annual: marriage, marriage of family member/close friend, divorce/separation, graduation (self or family member), start or termination of job (self or family member), change in job status (e.g., raise, promotion, demotion), departure of family member from home, change in schools or church, relocation to new area or new home, purchase of home, health problem or operation (self or significant others), injury/accident (self or significant others), financial difficulties, death of family member or significant other, vacation, victim of crime, natural disaster (hurricane, earthquake, flooding).

CPSIA information can be obtained
at www.ICGtesting.com
Printed in the USA
446575LV00001B/1
* 9 7 8 0 1 9 5 1 8 3 8 8 7 *